Tiny Tinkles Little Musicians Series

BOOK 6

Little Performers PLAY

F G A B

Created by Debra Krol

Pictures by Corinne Orazietti & Melanie Hawkins

This book is dedicated to
all the little people for inspiring me,
and all the BIG people for believing in me.

To request permission, or for school visits and book readings, please visit www.tinytinkles.com

ISBN (Paperback Perfect Bound): 978-1-990563-05-8

First Edition 2022

TIPS TO HELP YOU TEACH USING THIS BOOK

Welcome to the **Tiny Tinkles Little Musicians Series!** This 6th book in the Little Performers Collection will teach your little musician beginning notation for the notes, F, G, A and B in both the treble clef and the bass clef. Use the activity cards that are included to help your child become familiar with the location of the notes before beginning the songs. With a little practice, your child will be able to identify all four notes, play lots of games and create moments to explore the keys. Take time to listen and sing the animal sounds, character names and note names! Remember these key words: EXPLORE, LISTEN & PLAY....and your little musician will be set up for successful learning!

I recommend you introduce FGAB with fingers 1234 for your right hand, and 5432 in your left hand, but this book gives you the flexibility to introduce with other if you prefer.

Here's some more ideas to help you teach your little musician:

Keep a STEADY BEAT while you play the patterns and songs in this book.

SING while you play the notes! Your little musician will FEEL the beat and rythm of the music.

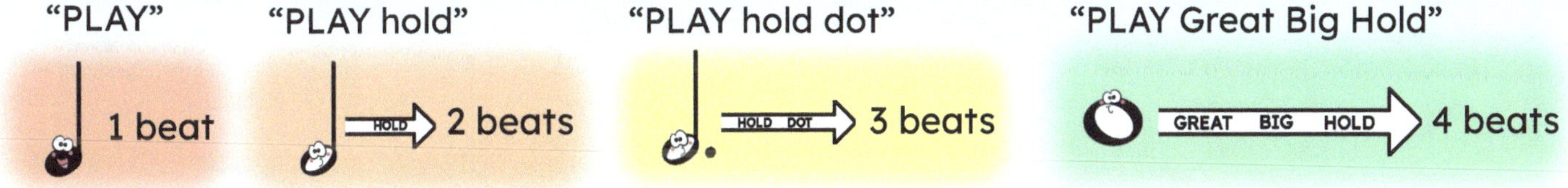

TIPS TO HELP YOU PRACTICE AND LEARN TOGETHER

- Ask questions like "is it a line or space"
- Count slowly before you begin
- Clap and count the beat before you begin
- Tap the notes and sing LEFT and RIGHT
- Circle patterns or common fingers
- Practice drawing the staff lines and notes
- Play and sing LEFT/RIGHT while you play
- Play and sing the WORDS while you play
- Try playing all the melodies hands together
- Try transposing to different hand positions

For videos, worksheets, teaching tips and more... please visit: www.tinytinkles.com

Today is an exciting day in

Tiny Tinkles Town!

Threezie is showing **Tina Treble** and **Bobby Bass** how to play her favorite **white keys!**

Threezie has **four** white keys.
Let's count them!

They are the notes **F, G, A,** and **B.**

Threezie loves playing **F, G, A, and B!**

She plays them down **low...**

And she plays them up **high!**

Then, **THREEZIE** leaps off the piano keys and finds **F, G, A, and B** in **Grammy's Treble Clef!**

F
G
A
B
F
G
A
B

Tina Treble sings and plays three beautiful **F's** with her **right hand.**

F
F
F
F

Then, **Tina Treble** moves up to the next white keys

and plays two **G's**, two **A's** and two beautiful **B's**!

Low notes are **Bobby Bass**'s favorite, so he plays a groovy low **F, G, A,** and **B** in **Grampy's Bass Clef.**

F G A B
FGAB

Playing piano is so much fun! **Bobby Bass** plays his pattern over and over again... **F, G, A, B... F, G, A, B...**

F
G
A
B

"Wiggle Friends...get ready to **wiggle and jiggle!"**

"Let's Play SONGS on F, G, A, and B!"

GAMES

1. MATCH the notation cards with the correct piano key.

2. SORT the cards into categories: Treble Clef notes and Bass Clef notes, F's, G's, A's, or B's, or into the same rhythmic patterns.

3. PLAY "I have, who has" or "Go fish."

4. PLAY the notes on the cards. Shuffle cards, place a few on the fallboard, and practice playing the patterns you see! Start with all the same note, then add new notes as you become more comfortable identifying them.

F
G
A
B

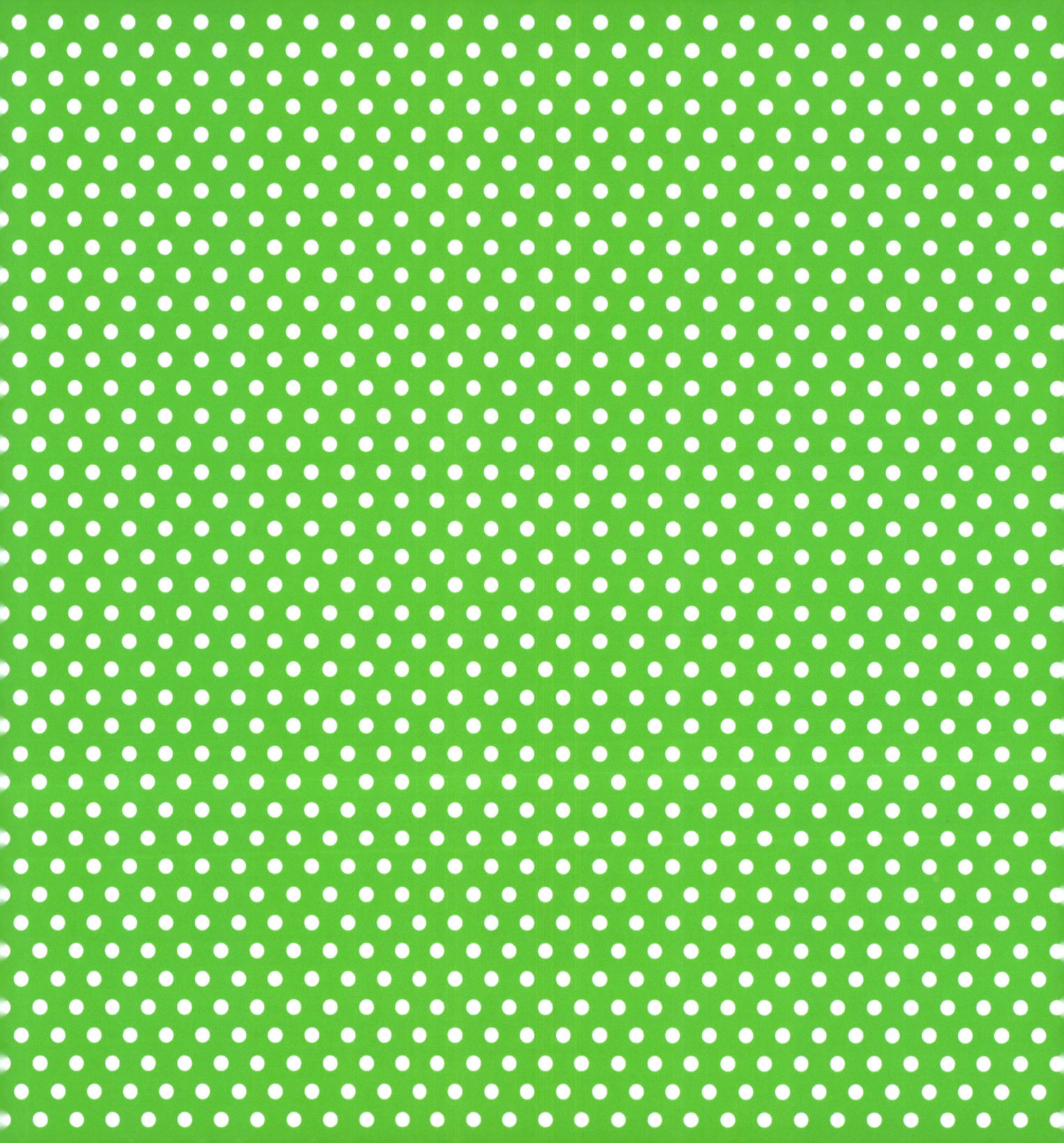

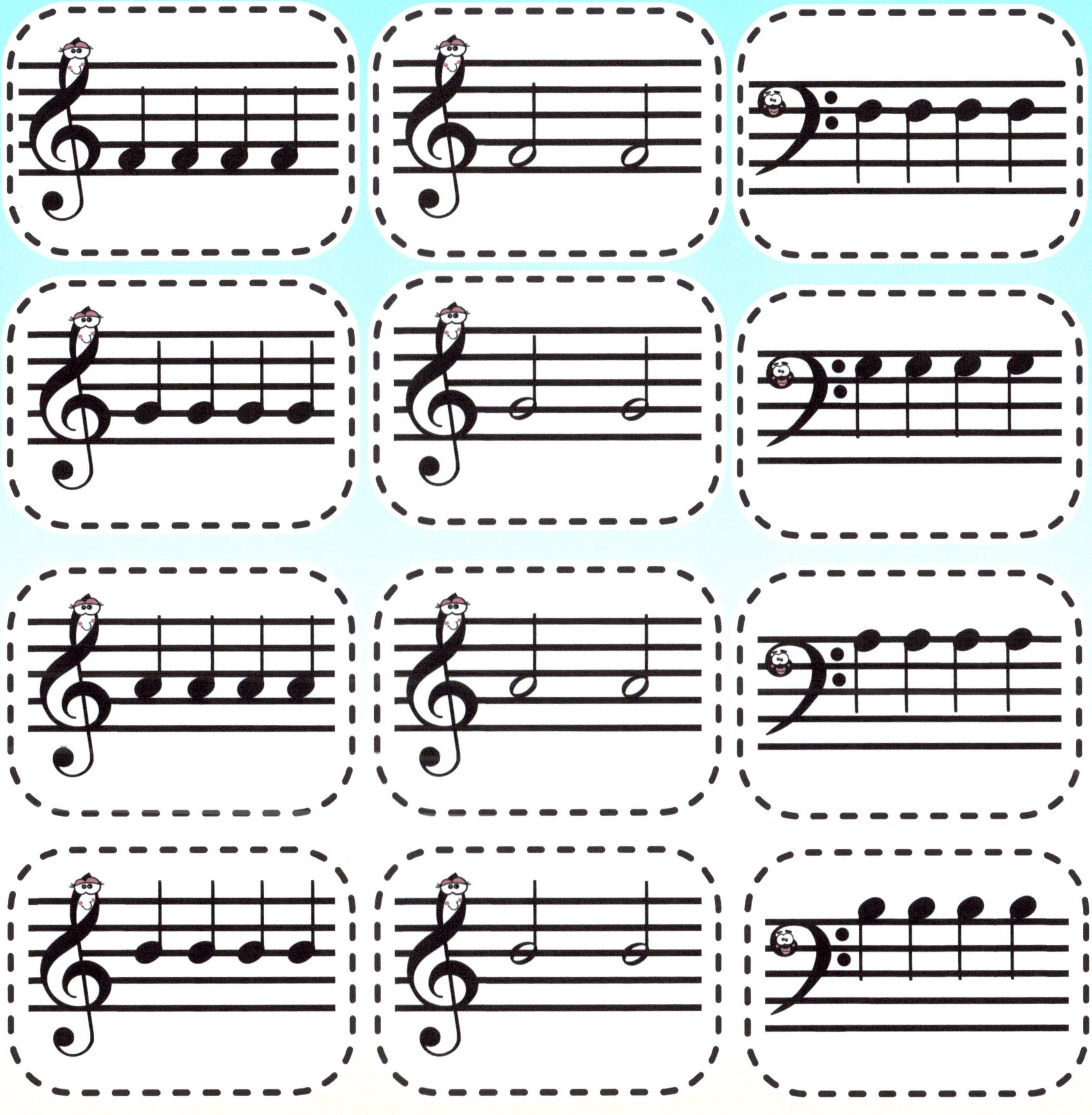

F

G

A

B

Connect with Your Child Through PLAY...

Find all of our Resources

Books, Videos, Printables, & more at

www.tinytinkles.com

Threezies White Keys

B	A	G	F
ROAR	CHOMP	MAA	RIBBIT

Silly Ghost!

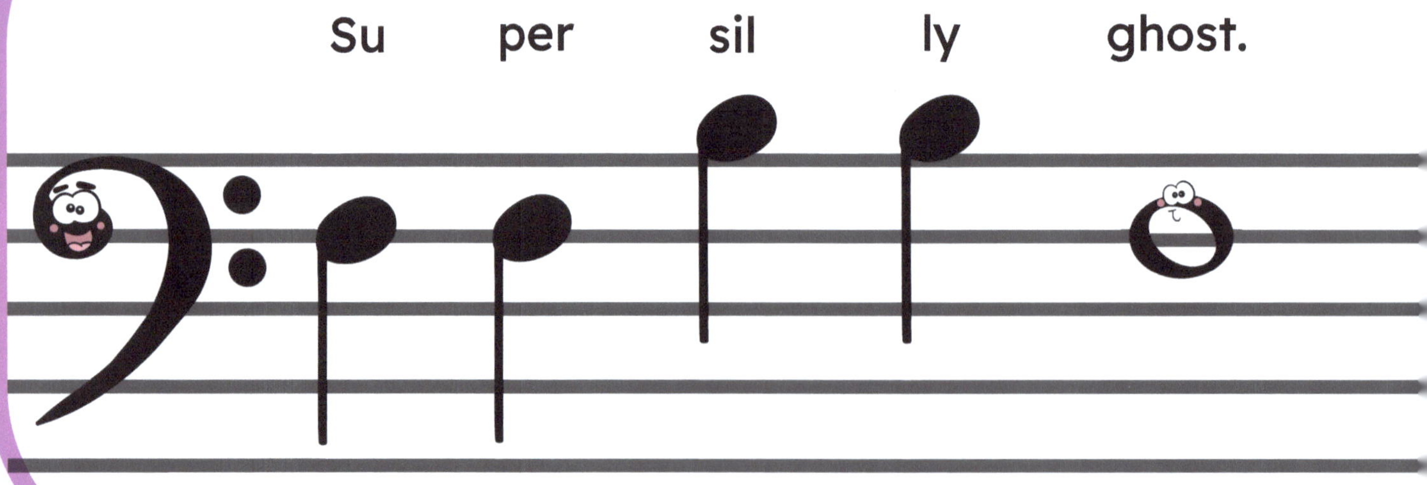

End with a **forte** BOO!

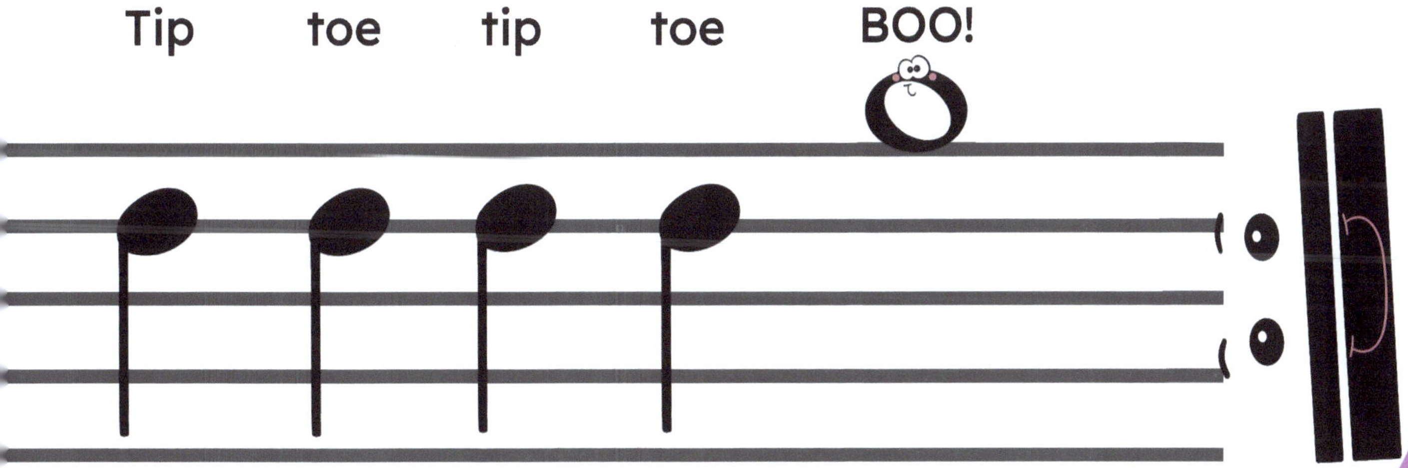

Sing and Play

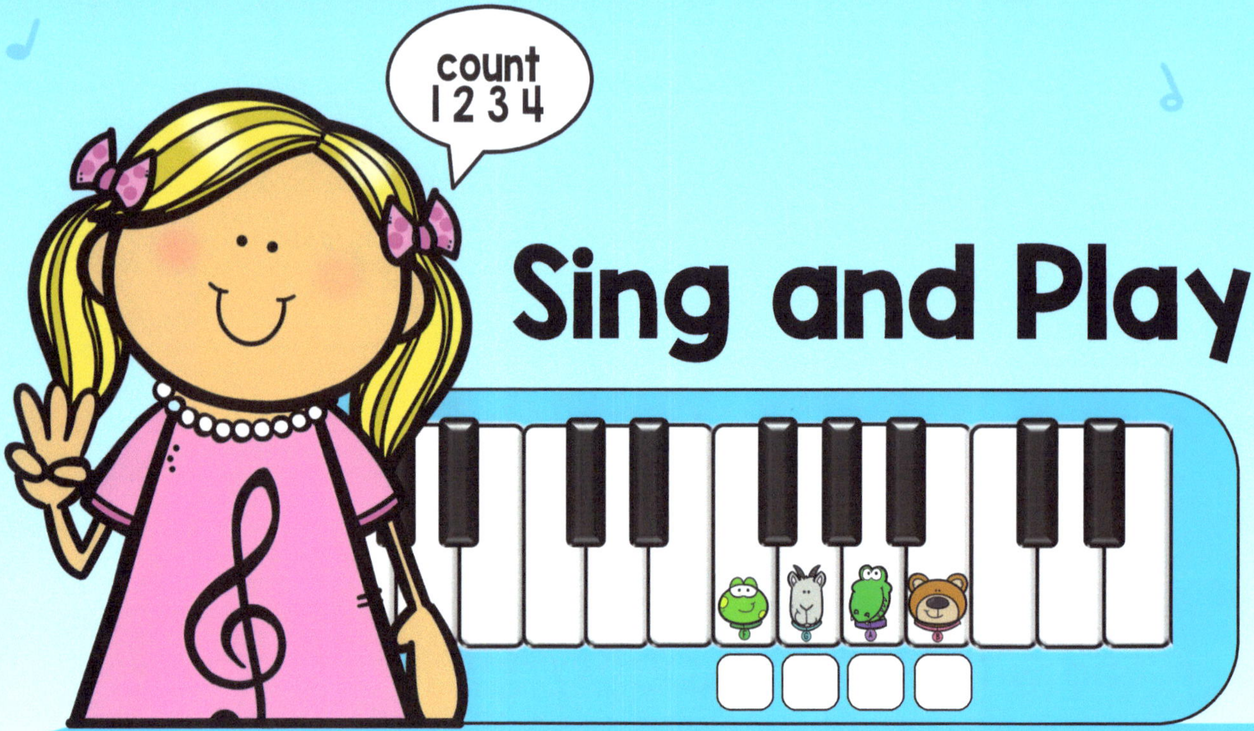
count
1 2 3 4

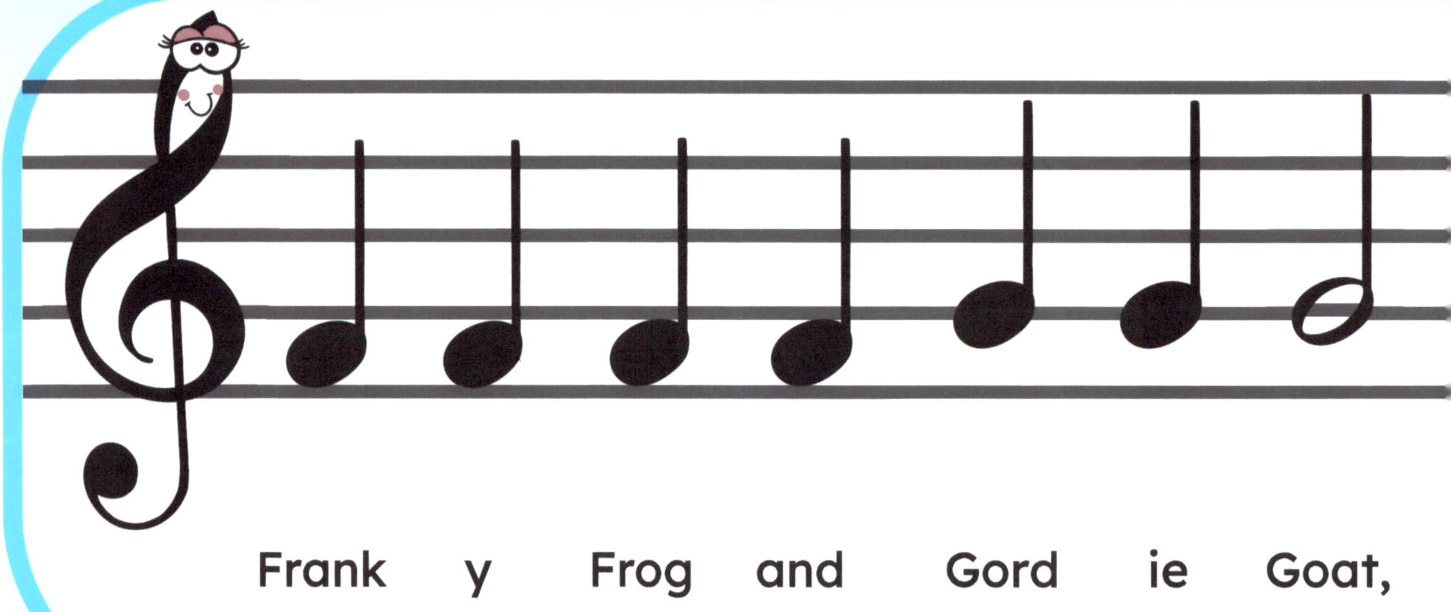
Frank y Frog and Gord ie Goat,

Maa!
G
F
Ribbit!

love to sing and play!

Donuts!

Would you like some do nuts?

count
1 2 3 4
WEEE!

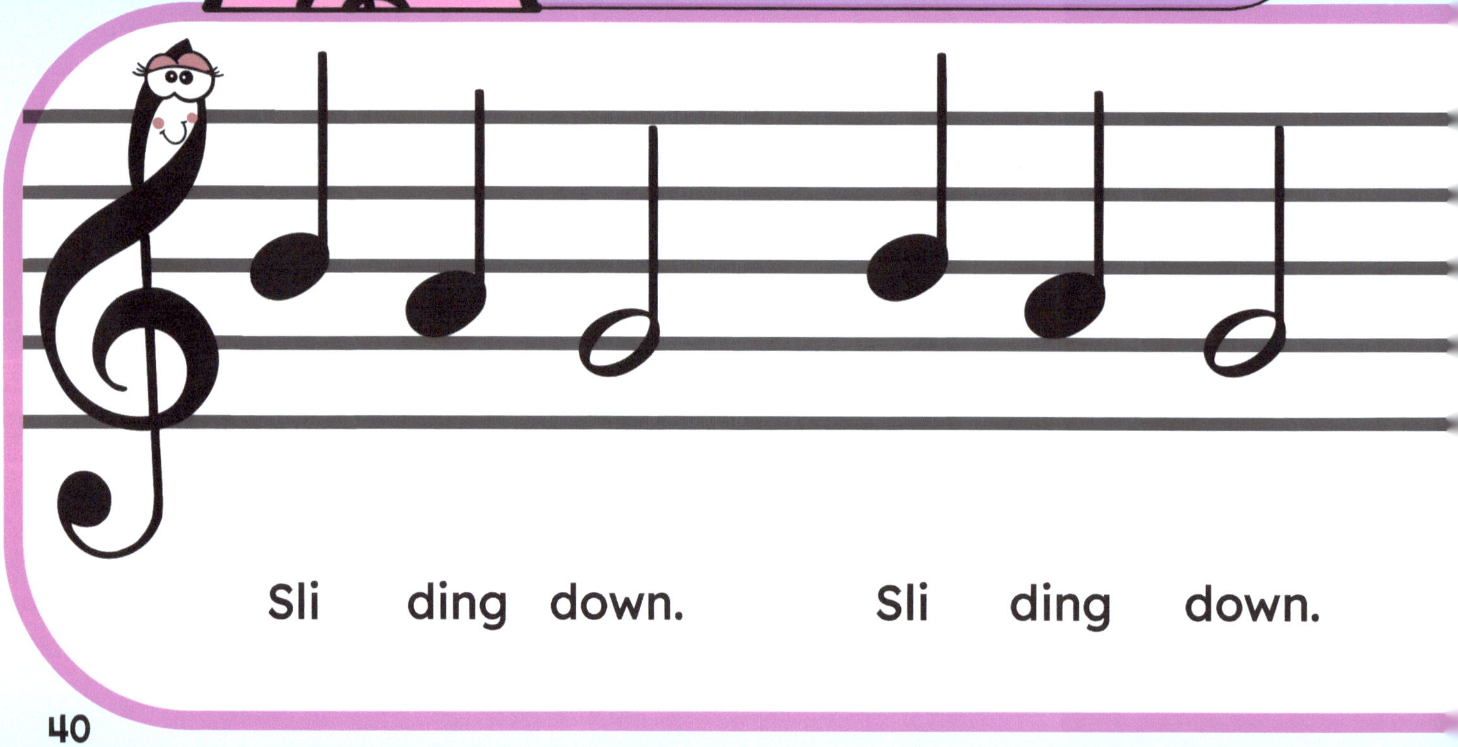
Sli ding down. Sli ding down.

Wee!
Frank ky Frog sings WEEE!

Tweet!

End with a great big TWEET!

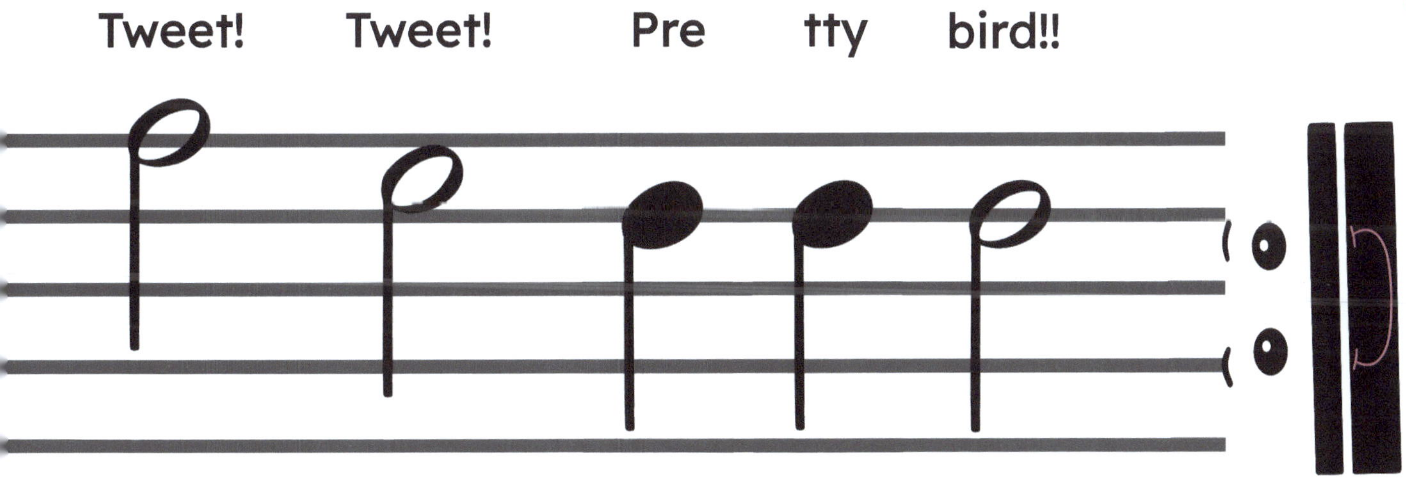

Mister Moon

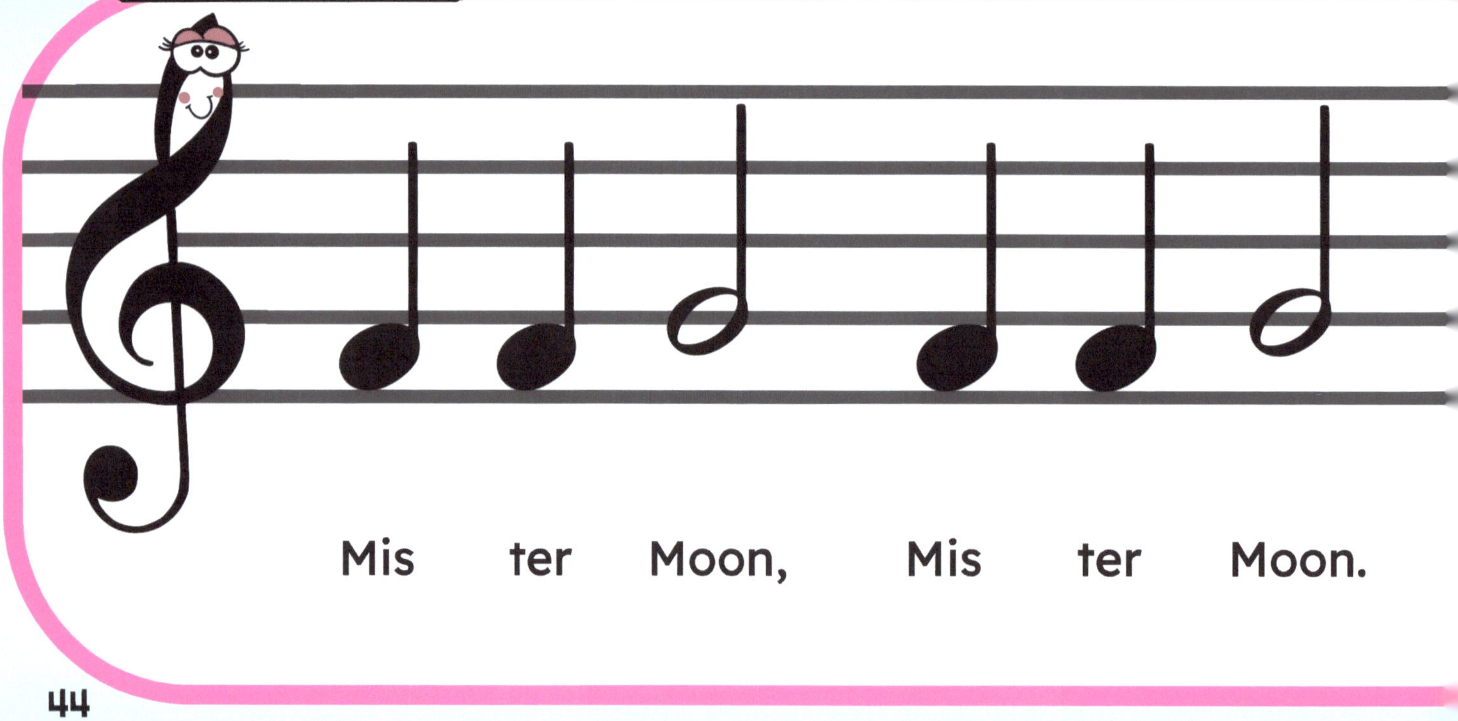

Good night Mis ster Moon.

Butterfly

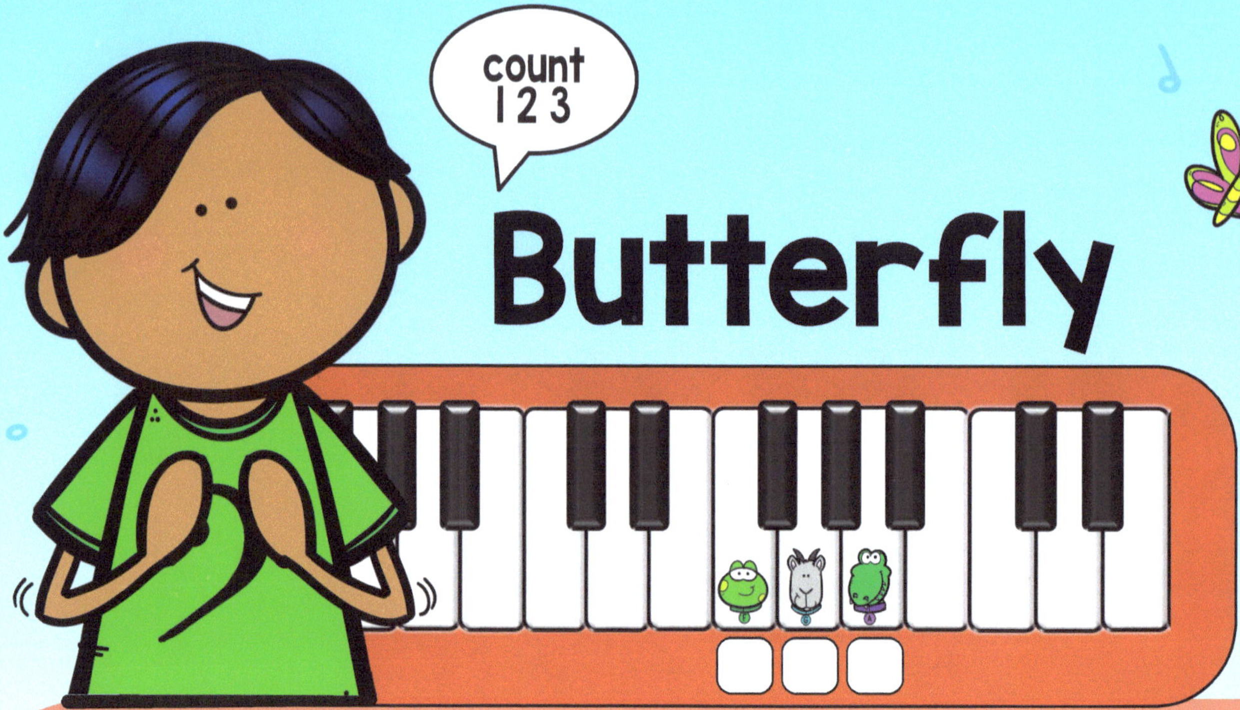
count
1 2 3

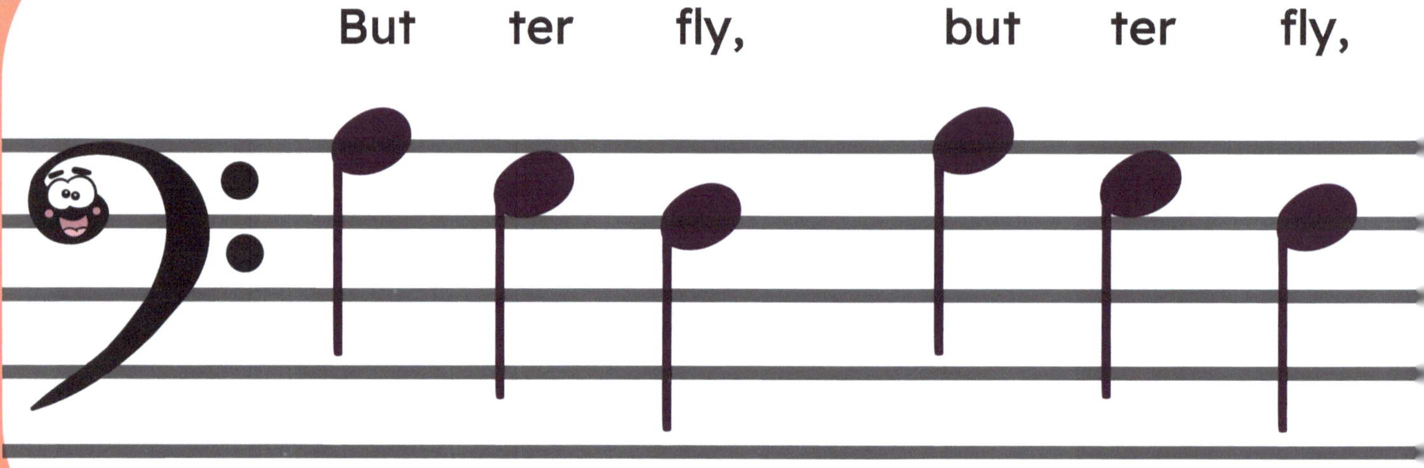
But ter fly, but ter fly,

fly
ing
so
high
Woosh!

Bumble Bee

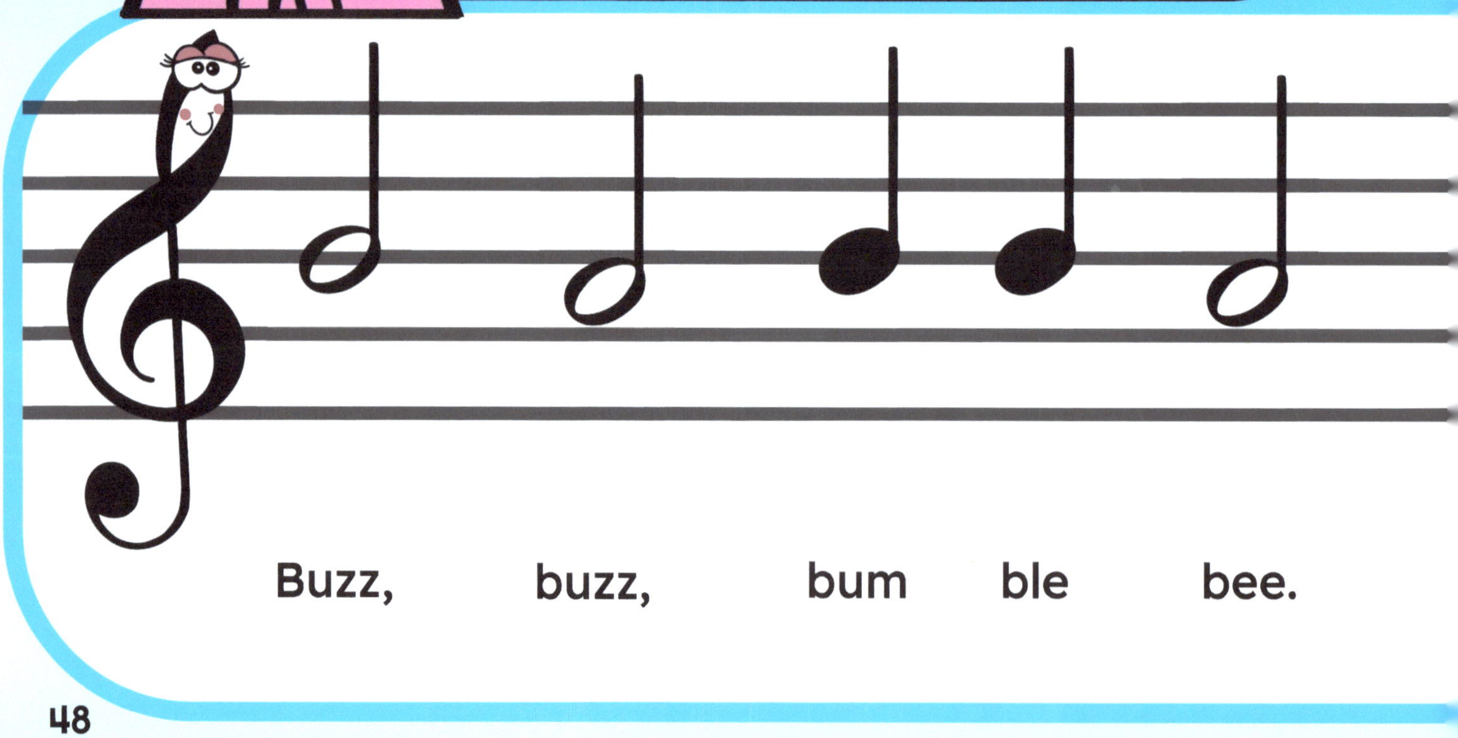

End with a big Bzz!!

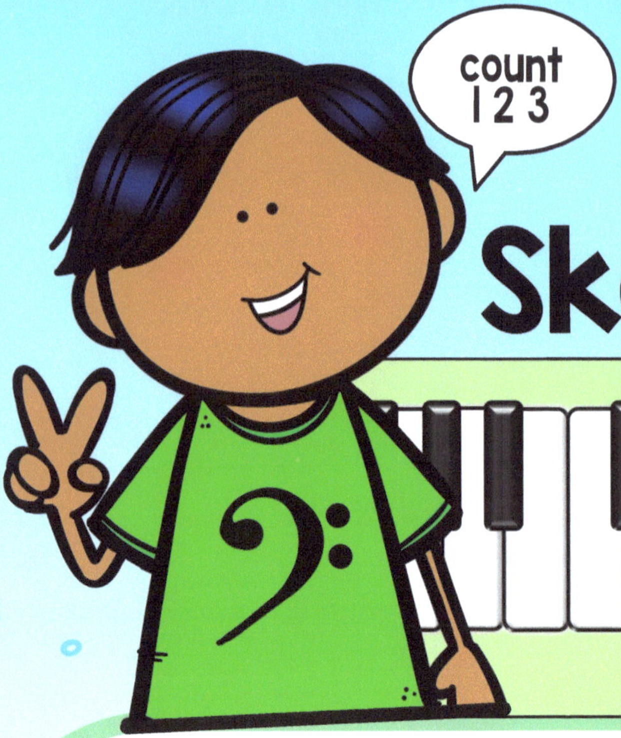
count
1 2 3

Skateboard

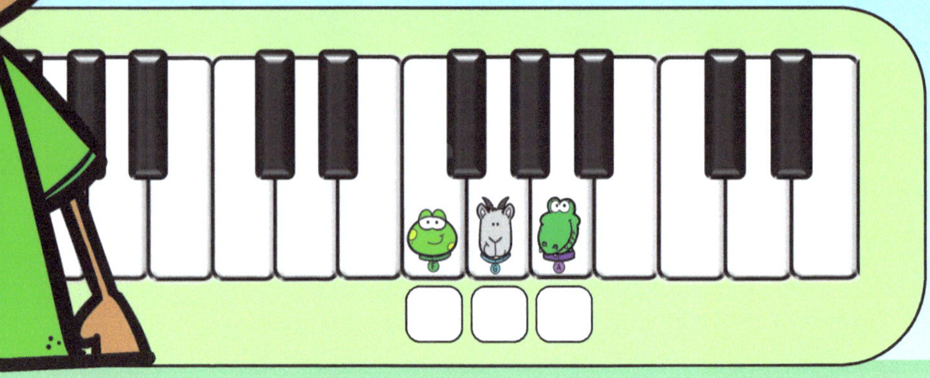

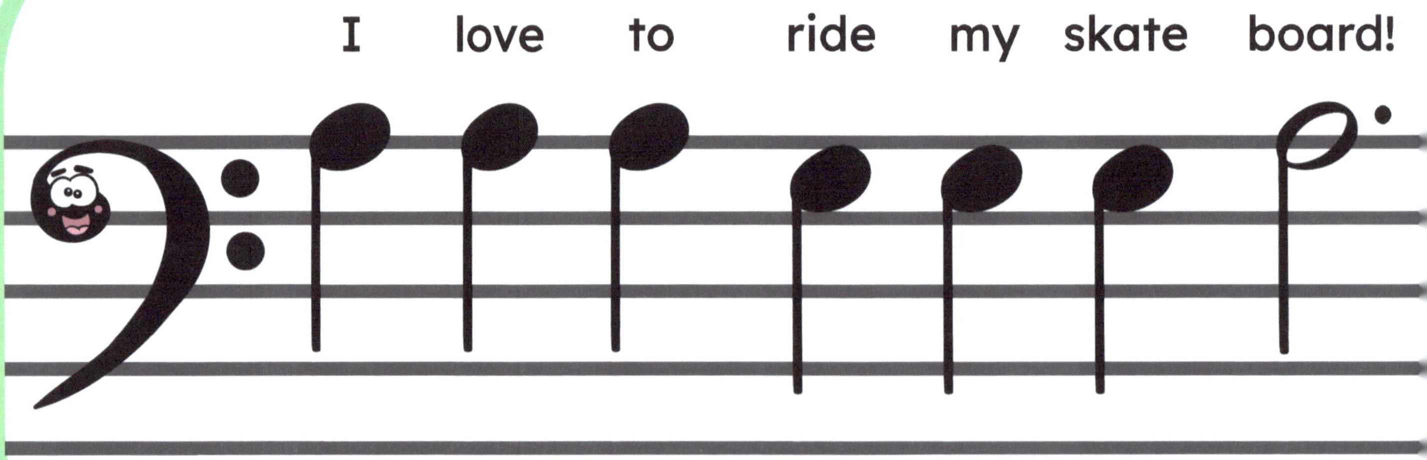
I love to ride my skate board!

wahoo!

I love to go re ally FAST!

Let's Dance!

be
her
dance
part
ner?

count
1 2 3 4

Floating Clouds

Floa ting clouds, floa ting clouds.

Slow ly drif ting in the sky.

Choo Choo Train

Let's go and ride on my train.

Love our Books?

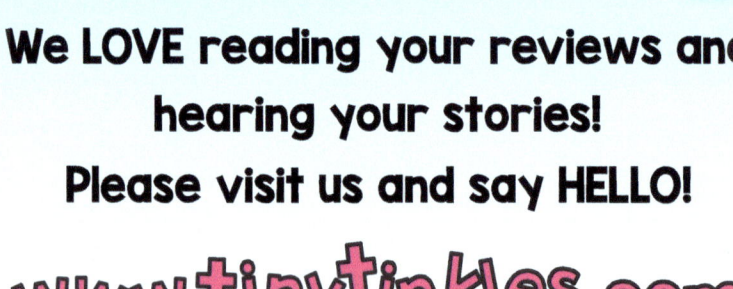

We LOVE reading your reviews and hearing your stories!

Please visit us and say HELLO!

www.tinytinkles.com

CONGRATULATIONS!

____

Student's Name

has completed Little Performers Level 6
in the Tiny Tinkles Little Musician Series.

LEVEL
6

____

Teacher

____

Date

www.ingramcontent.com/pod-product-compliance
Lightning Source LLC
Chambersburg PA
CBHW041553120626
46551CB00002B/189
9781990563058